# Contents

©2013, from *Wildflower Album: Appliqué & Embroidery Patterns* (AQS, 2000)

# Introduction

The designs in this book can be used to make a single block of your favorite flower for a pillow, a small wallhanging, or a medallion center for a larger wallhanging. They can also be combined with other blocks to make a whole quilt of the size you desire. The blocks can be combined with sashing and borders to create a variety of sizes. Plan your quilt size on graph paper and choose the number of blocks you want to include. By choosing your own blocks, setting, and size, your finished quilt will be uniquely yours.

Each finished block is 12" x 12". For each block, cut a 14" square to compensate for the drawing up of the fabric and the fraying of the edges during the appliqué process. After the appliqué is finished, the block is trimmed to 12½" x12½". The number of blocks needed to complete your project will determine the amount of material needed. Be generous in the amount you buy. It is better to have too much than too little. Any leftovers can be used in your flower and leaf appliqué.

For each of these 14 block patterns, a color photograph and a full-sized pattern, with tips on fabric selection and appliqué techniques, are provided. Also included are descriptions and characteristics of each of these flowers so they will become familiar, alive, and a joy to sew.

# General Instructions

## Gather supplies and tools

**Background fabric:** I use 100% cotton fabric of good quality and even weave. This can be light or dark. It can be plain, have a small-scale print, or have a mottled background. If a dark fabric is used, the flowers and leaves need to be light or bright to show. If a color is used, keep in mind the color of the flowers. A medium blue flower on a medium blue background will be lost.

**Appliqué fabric:** Also use 100% cotton for the flowers and leaves. Cotton is the easiest fabric to work with. Blends, rayon, and silk ravel and are difficult to turn under to make smooth curved edges. Flowers and leaves in real life have texture and movement, so it is best to choose fabrics with prints, geometrics, and florals, both large and small.

**Thread:** If you are experienced in appliqué and have a favorite thread, by all means use it. The thread should match the appliqué piece as closely as possible. I prefer 100% cotton that is sometimes called machine embroidery thread.

**Needles:** For appliqué, Sharps and Straw needles are recommended. Straw needles are longer than Sharps and have a narrower shank. The higher the number, the smaller the needle. Some quilters prefer a size #11 Straw needle for intricate hand appliqué, but I cannot adjust to their length, so I use a Sharp size #11. These are smaller than the Straw needles and only a bit longer than the Betweens that I use for quilting. Sharps have a narrow shank and do not leave holes in the fabric.

**Pins:** I use silk pins with glass heads. These are very sharp and thin. They do not leave holes in the fabric as large pins will, and their glass heads make them easy to remove.

**Thimble:** I use a standard metal thimble with a small rim. Try several types to discover what works best for you.

**Scissors:** For appliqué work, I use three different scissors. I use two pairs of 5" scissors, one for cutting paper and plastic, and one for cutting fabric. This small size is handy for going around curves and cutting small patterns. The sharp points are useful for snipping curves and notches. I use appliqué scissors for trimming away excess fabric in the back of the appliqué. These have one narrow blade and one semicircular wide blade to minimize the danger of accidentally cutting into the appliqué.

**Marking pens and pencils:** There are many on the market. One main thing to remember when choosing a marking tool is to test each one on the fabric to be used. Wash the fabric, and if the mark comes out, you can use it. If it doesn't come out, try another marker. Sometimes a marker will wash out of one fabric but not another. ***Test!***

If I use a light background, I like to mark my patterns with a .5-mm mechanical quilters' pencil. It is always sharp, never smears, makes a very fine line, and washes out. Regular lead pencils dull easily, and the softer the lead, the more they smear, and they usually do not wash out. If using a dark fabric, I prefer a white charcoal pencil that can be sharpened. Charcoal can be brushed out or wiped away with a damp cloth. Do not iron the pieces until the markings have been removed. The iron will set the markings.

## Prepare background squares

Thoroughly wash and rinse all the fabrics to be used. Remove fabrics from the dryer before they are completely dry and iron them with a steam iron.

Cut as many squares 14" x 14" (to finish 12" x 12") as needed. As these are cut, mark the top of each one with a small T to keep the grain line running in the same direction.

Spray the background squares with starch before you mark the pattern on them. The starch gives the fabric body, makes it easier to mark, and the fabric will not wrinkle as you mark.

## Make a master pattern

Draw your master pattern on paper. I use a drawing tablet from an art-supply store for this. Each sheet can be torn out as needed. Freezer paper can be used, but it comes in rolls, which is inconvenient. Use a fine felt, permanent black pen to mark your pattern on the paper. Be sure to include the numbers for appliqué sequence on the master pattern.

If the background fabric has a print or it is dark, a light box or window may be necessary to see the pattern through the fabric. Center your background fabric over the pattern and lightly mark the whole pattern on the fabric.

## Prepare appliqués

Using a pencil, draw around each piece of the flower pattern on the dull side of a piece of freezer paper and number each piece. If only one fabric is used, the flower will look flat, and you will see no distinction between the petals. Within a daisy, you can have several shades, tints, and values of the same hue. Remember that dark colors recede and light colors advance. Change the values of your green stems and leaves, too, so you can see each one distinctly as you would in nature. Cut each pattern piece from the freezer paper exactly on the line. Do not add turn-under allowances.

To help choose the position of the pattern on the fabric, I use a window template. From an office supply store, I buy inexpensive note pads, about 4" x 5". I can tear off a sheet, draw a leaf or flower petal in the center of it and cut it out to make my window. When I position the window on the fabric, I can see exactly how the leaf or petal will look when it is finished. Then I position the freezer-paper pattern on that area on the fabric. Iron the freezer-paper pattern, shiny side down, on the top of the desired fabric. Use a medium iron, no steam necessary, and a firm board. If the ironing board is too soft, the freezer paper will not adhere.

Using a water-soluble marker, mark around each piece on your chosen fabrics. Cut out the pieces with generous ¼" turn-under allowances. On inside curves, clip every ⅛" to ¼" along the entire curve so the allowances will lie flat. On outside curves, you may want to trim closer or make tiny notches with scissors or pinking shears so you will not have any pleats or puckers on the underside. To keep all the cut pieces organized, place them in a pile in numerical order with #1 on top.

## Position and sew appliqués

For each piece, starting with piece #1, use your thumbnail and forefinger to turn under the allowance and crease the fabric on the sewing line around the entire pattern piece. Remove the freezer paper. With cotton fabric, the crease will remain and the allowance will easily needle-turn with your appliqué stitch. Position the piece on the background block. I use one pin to hold the piece. If necessary, I clip and trim the allowances close to the fold line as I sew. With tiny and close appliqué stitches, I am able to sew sharp points and gentle, smooth curves. When the appliqué is finished, if the piece is large, cut away the background fabric from under it, leaving a ¼" allowance. This trimming will keep the piece from becoming too heavy or bulky, and it is easier to quilt through a single layer.

## Remove markings and press

After the block has been appliquéd, wash out any markings that show before pressing. Otherwise, the heat will set them. I first press from the right side. Using the tip of a dry iron, press from the center of each appliqué piece to the outer edge.

## Finish the block

After pressing, you can embellish the flowers and leaves with embroidery. On a soft, padded surface, press the block again, this time from the back to keep the embroidery from becoming flat. Block the finished square and trim it to 12½" x 12½", which includes seam allowances.

# American Waterlily

## 46 appliqué pieces

### Color notes:

Use a rich, hand-dyed or marbled green for the leaves and a darker green for the stems. The flowers can be made in several shades of white, pale pink, or rose. Use yellow embroidery floss and French knots for the stamens. The veins in the leaves can be emphasized by the quilting pattern.

## Construction tips:

Sew stem 1 first. Sew leaf 2 next, but leave the lower part unsewn until stem 3 has been appliquéd in place. Then finish leaf 2.

Also called Sweet-Scented Waterlily and the Water Queen, this flower is so beautiful that people do not consider it to be a wildflower. It is a hardy perennial with a heavy perfume that beckons bees and butterflies. The flowers are multi-petaled, about five to six inches in diameter. They are usually white but can also be pale pink or rose with numerous yellow stamens. Each flower rises on a one- to two-foot-tall stem. The leaves can be up to two feet across and are platter-shaped, thick, and leathery. They have many veins, are dark green on top and purplish red underneath. The plant floats on shallow, slow-running streams, or in ponds, bays, and protected coves. The blossom opens only in the morning sun and closes in the afternoon. They last three or four days and bloom all summer.

# Bee Balm

## 59 appliqué pieces

### Color notes:

The leaves, stems, and pieces 35 and 48 are gray green. Use two or three greens for interest and contrast. Choose a rich scarlet for the flower petals. A marbled fabric or several different red fabrics can be used. Make piece 18 a darker red than the petals.

A member of the mint family, this plant was known as Oswego Tea, but Native Americans called it O-Gee-Chee, which means flaming flower. It has a sturdy stem and grows up to four feet tall. With its scarlet red color and great height, it makes quite a show against the woods and thickets during the summer and early fall blooming season. The leaves are fragrant, fuzzy, and gray green. The flower heads are flamboyant and two to three inches in diameter. They are constantly visited by bees, butterflies, and ruby-throated hummingbirds. The needle-like bill of the hummingbird helps to pollinate the flowers. The Oswego Indians drank a tea made from the leaves and used it as a medicine. After the Boston Tea Party caused a shortage of imported tea, Bee Balm leaves were used as a substitute.

# Birdfoot Violet

## 40 appliqué pieces

### Color notes:

Use medium greens for the stems and leaves. The violets are pale blue-lavender. A mottled or hand-dyed fabric will make attractive flowers. Use bright orange for pieces 20, 26, and 39.

This is one of about 500 members of the violet family. All bloom in the spring, and all have similar flower petal arrangements. The name refers to the shape of the leaf, which resembles a bird's foot. The broad, flat flower petals are pale blue-lavender, sometimes striped with purple, with bright orange stamens. The flowers are about one and a half inches across on two- to six-inch stalks. The deeply notched medium green leaves grow from the base of the plant. This violet thrives in sandy soil on prairies, along embankments, and in eastern woodland openings. These hardy perennials flower from mid to late spring.

*Photo courtesy of Jacqueline Donnelly*

# Evening Primrose

## 43 appliqué pieces

### Color notes:

Choose a medium green for the leaves and purplish brown for the stems. The flowers are a bright yellow. Use two or more fabrics for contrast and deep yellow embroidery floss for the centers, including the French knots.

The Evening Primrose is a native of our American continent, but it was cultivated in seventeenth century England. The roots were said to be wholesome and nutritious when boiled, and the tender shoots were sometimes used for salads. Today, the oil of the primrose is sold in health food stores and is said to have curative powers. The leaves are long and narrow. The flowers consist of clusters of bright yellow, saucer-shaped petals, about two to three inches across on stout, purplish brown stems. The flowers, which open in the evening, have a strong fragrance and are a favorite of moths. Honeybees and bumblebees visit the flowers in the morning before they close and wither in the noonday sun. They grow in dry, sandy soil and flower July to September.

# Golden Thin-leaf Sunflower

## 38 appliqué pieces

### Color notes:

Use a medium green with two or three shades for the leaves. Three or more shades of golden yellow will be needed for the petals to distinguish one from another. The center can be brownish green or brown. A three-dimensional effect can be obtained by sewing French knots in the disks.

## Construction tips:

The stalk, piece 14, is cut all in one piece and appliquéd after the leaves.

The Sunflower is the state flower of Kansas, and although it is considered a prairie flower, Native Americans cultivated it 300 years ago along the shore of Lake Huron. All parts of the plant were used: the stalk for rope and textile fiber, the leaves for fodder, the seeds for oil and food, and the petals for yellow dye. Lewis and Clark recorded Sunflowers on their journey along the Missouri River in Montana.

Today, throughout Europe and America, the plant is widely cultivated, and the seeds have multiple uses as an oil and food for both humans and animals. It can grow from two to eight feet tall on strong, erect stems with a large flower head that blooms mid to late summer. The flower has bright golden yellow petals, three to eight inches across, which surround a large brown or greenish brown disk. The leaves are medium green and three to twelve inches in length.

# Jack-in-the-Pulpit

## 15 appliqué pieces

### Color notes:

Use several shades of medium green for the leaves and a deeper shade for stems 7 and 13. Leaves 8 and 14 need to be appliquéd after the stems are in place. For the flower, use a muted stripe with maroon or purple and green, if it can be found. The Jack, piece 11, is a bright yellow.

A member of the Arum family, Jack-in-the-Pulpit is an intriguing plant because of its flower shape and color. It brings to mind the elves and spirits of the woodlands. There is even a poem about this flower:

*Jack-in-the-Pulpit, Preaches today,*
*Under the green trees, Just over the way.*
*Come hear what his reverence rises to say.*

*…Anonymous*

This woodland plant can grow to three feet tall, but 12 to 18 inches is the norm. It has three-part leaves that overshadow the hooded flower. The two-to three-inch bright yellow "Jack" arises from the center of the plant. The strange-shaped hood over the Jack is striped green and reddish purple, with a deep maroon or purple underneath. This plant grows from the Midwest to the East Coast.

# Lupine

## 91 appliqué pieces

### Color notes:

Choose a rich green for the leaves and a deeper green for the stems. For the flowers, use several shades of a rich blue with the lightest shades on top. For the little flower stems, use two or three strands of matching green embroidery floss and embroider them with the stem stitch.

The Lupine is a member of the bean family. Texans call it Bluebonnet because the flowers seem to completely cover the hillsides like a bonnet of blue. These flowers are also called Buffalo Clover because they grow wild in masses where the buffalo roamed and churned the seeds into the soil. The stems of this plant grow eight to twenty-four inches tall with whorls of half-inch pea-like flowers covering the tops of the stems. The flower is a rich blue with the upper portion of the bloom usually a pale blue or white. The leaves, which radiate from a central point, are made up of seven to nine leaflets, which rotate to follow the sun. The plants grow in a semi-arid grassland environment and need sun and well-drained soil. They bloom from mid summer into early autumn.

## Construction tips:

Although there are many pieces in this pattern, it is not difficult if the colors are planned and the pieces are appliquéd in numerical order.

# Solomon's Seal

## 54 appliqué pieces

### Color notes:

Use two or more shades of light green for the leaves and stems. The underside of the leaf is darker than the top. Use greenish white for the flowers and a deep navy or blue-black for the berries.

This flower is a member of the Lily family. It's uncertain how the flower got its name. Some people think that the patterns on the underground rhizomes resemble King Solomon's seal. Others think the name comes from the Six-pointed Star pattern that can be seen in the rhizome's cross-section. The plant grows one to three feet tall with graceful, leafy stems. The light green leaves are oblong and smooth, and they grow alternately on the stem. The bell-shaped flowers are greenish white and droop in pairs beneath the leaves. As the flowers ripen, they produce a blue-black berry that is about one-fourth inch in diameter. In the spring, the tender shoots can be boiled and served like asparagus. Native Americans used the starchy root as food. Neither the flowers nor the berries are particularly showy, but the grace of the plant is a most decorative feature of the spring woodlands.

## Construction tips:

Leave a section of stem 15 free until berry stem 17 can be sewn.

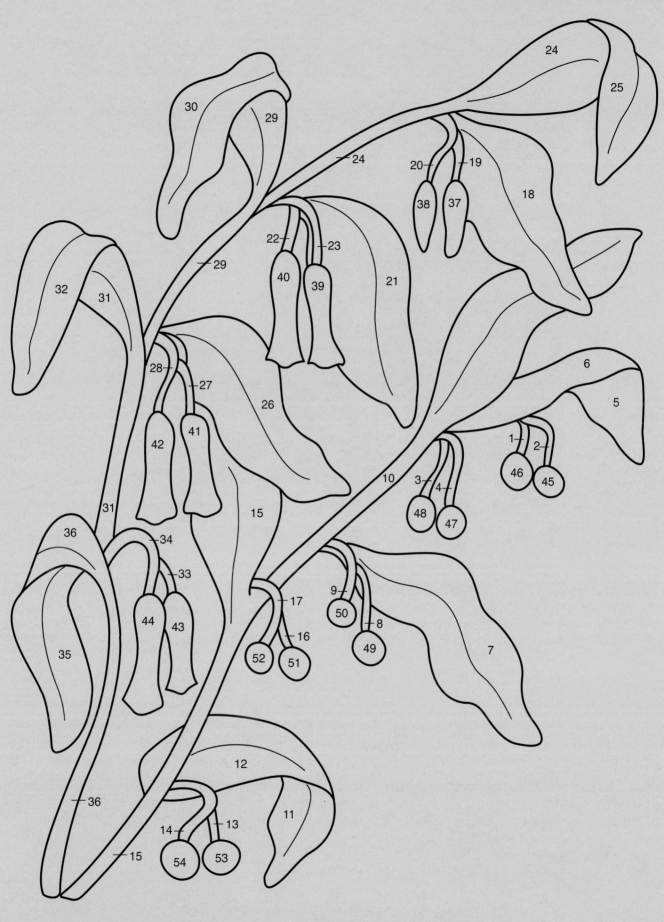

# Swamp Rose Mallow

## 32 appliqué pieces

### Color notes:

Use medium green for the leaves with a deeper green for the underleaf. The stems are a deep brownish green. The flowers are true pink. Select two shades, marbled or hand dyed, to distinguish between petals, with a deeper pink for the underside of the petals. Use bright yellow embroidery floss and French knots for the stamens.

The Swamp Rose Mallow is in the same family as the hibiscus, okra, cotton, hollyhock, and rose of Sharon. The root of the Wild Marsh Mallow was used medicinally in the seventeenth and eighteenth centuries and was said to cure an assortment of ills. These plants grow along the marshes of rivers or the ocean on the eastern coast, from Massachusetts to Florida. The plant grows three to seven feet tall. The flowers are large, four to seven inches across, with five petals and numerous yellow stamens in the center. The flowers, which flower in August and September, are pink with a deeper pink on the underside. The leaves are slightly heart shaped.

# Wild Ginger

## 10 appliqué pieces

### Color notes:

Use marbled fabric of olive or medium green for the leaves. The same or a different green can be used for the stem. Pieces 3 and 4 can be a medium brown. Select a brownish purple for the flowers with a darker fabric for the center. Sew French knots of a deeper shade in piece 10 for the seeds. The leaf veins can be quilted.

Wild Ginger gets its name from the underground rhizomes that have a ginger-like aroma and taste. The flower is difficult to find because it opens so close to the ground, and it has a somber, purplish brown color, frequently concealed by leaves. The leaves are five to seven inches across and are heart- or kidney-shaped. They are thick, velvety, and heavily veined. Each plant has two leaves with a single flower at the base of the leaf stalk. The one- to two-inch flower has no real petals, but there are three brownish or brownish purple lobes. The flower contains a vessel filled with many seeds that burst open when ripe. The plants grow in rich woodlands from Canada to North Carolina and bloom only in the early spring.

# Wild Iris

## 37 appliqué pieces

### Color notes:

For realistic flowers, use an assortment of greens, making sure the underside of the leaves are a deeper shade. The flower and the buds are lavender blue, with yellow for pieces 26, 30, 36, and 37.

Also called Blue Flag, this flower is a relative of the domestic or garden iris. It is one of the most regal of all wildflowers. Although it is called blue, the wild variety has more of a lavender tinge. The leaves are a rich green, long, and sword shaped. The flower stalks grow straight up and over the leaves. They both arise from creeping rhizomes that are poisonous. Each stalk bears one or two flowers that have a distinct three-part arrangement. The three top petals point skyward and the three lower petals, called falls, droop downward. Between the petals and the falls are the lip and the stamens. This unusual arrangement ensures cross-pollination. The flowers, which last three to six days, grow in the wetlands of the northern part of North America and do best in partial shade. They bloom from spring to mid summer. This plant is undemanding in the garden and most rewarding.

# Wild Sweet William

## 71 appliqué pieces

### Color notes:

Use a yellow-green for the leaves and a deeper green for the stems. For the flowers, select rich pinks of different fabrics or shades so that the petals will be distinct from each other. For the centers, use bright yellow embroidery floss and French knots.

Wild Sweet William is also called Meadow Phlox and Pinks. These are ancient flowers that came to the United States from Britain. It is not known how the name came about, but some say it was from Saint William, whose feast day is the end of June when the flowers first bloom. The plant has stout six- to 18-inch stems. The leaves are shiny yellow-green, and they are scattered on the stems rather than paired. The three-fourths-inch flowers, with five broad petals, can be found in bright pink, purple, or red. They remain open six to eight days from late June to September and are pollinated by butterflies.

## Construction tips:

Although there are 71 pieces in this pattern, it is not difficult if care is taken to appliqué each piece in the order given.

# Wind Poppy

## 30 appliqué pieces

### Color notes:

Use several shades of green to distinguish between leaves. Stems can be the same color, but a different shade from leaves. When choosing fabric for the petals, pieces 5, 7, 15, 17, and 30 need to be a lighter shade. The centers can be a deep purple.

The common Poppy is sometimes called Corn Poppy because it germinates and thrives in freshly turned soil. In ancient times, the dried petals were used medicinally because they contain a soothing substance. It is not the same as the narcotic opium, which is derived from the Opium Poppy. The Corn Poppy is scarlet red, but the Wind Poppy can be apricot or coral in color. Poppies are easy to grow but difficult to transplant or move, so be sure to throw the seeds where they are to grow. The plant is bare stemmed with deeply cleft leaves, which are dense and close to the ground. The flowers have four broad apricot, coral, or orange-red petals with dark purple at the center. They are fragile and do not make good cut flowers.

# Wood Lily

## 27 appliqué pieces

### Color notes:

The leaves are medium green. Use a darker green for the underside and the stem. Choose several shades of bright orange or orange-red for the flower petals, with deeper shades for undersides. Embroider the stamens with black floss.

The Wood Lily is known by many names: Turks Cap Lily, Leopard Lily, Wild Red Lily, and Flame Lily. This is one of the few lily species with flowers that point upward. There are gaps between the petals, allowing rainwater to drain out. The flowers usually have one or two blooms on top of an eight- to 36-inch stem. The leaves are arranged in a whorl, or circular cluster, around the stem. The roots of these hardy perennials arise from a deep-seated, white scaly bulb, and new bulbs are formed at the sides of the mature bulb each year. The petals range from orange to bright orange-red, but all have deep purple, almost black, spots on the petals, thus the common name Leopard Lily. A few of the species in this family will grow in moist or swampy ground. Most grow in relatively dry prairies. They tolerate light shade but need full sun for a part of each day.

# Wood Lily

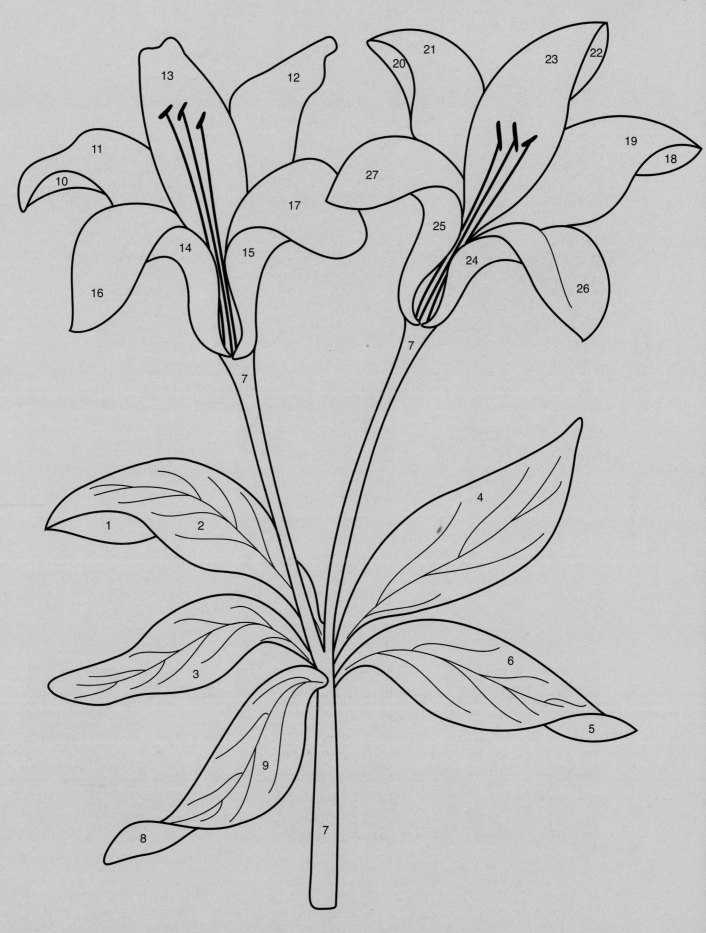

# More Love to Quilt Books

This is only a small selection of books available from Love to Quilt. Look for them at your local bookseller, fabric store, quilt shop, or public library.

**8-Pointed & Feathered STARS**
2 Fun & Fabulous Quilts
Gail Searl

#1284 ............................ $12.95

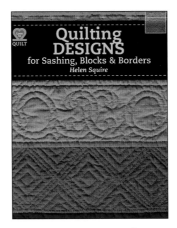

**Quilting DESIGNS**
for Sashing, Blocks & Borders
Helen Squire

#1286 ............................ $12.95

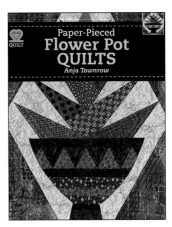

Paper-Pieced **Flower Pot QUILTS**
Anja Townrow

#1288 ............................ $12.95

Quilts That Celebrate **SPRING & SUMMER**
Karen Combs, Bethany S. Reynolds & Joan Shay

#1292 ............................ $12.95

**DOLLHOUSE QUILTS**
Tina M. Gravatt

#1290 ............................ $12.95

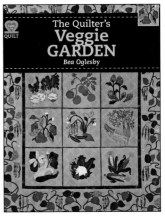

The Quilter's **Veggie GARDEN**
Bea Oglesby

#1287 ............................ $12.95

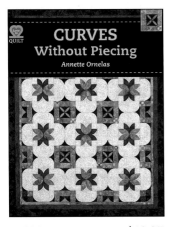

**CURVES Without Piecing**
Annette Ornelas

#1293 ............................ $12.95

**SEW STARS!**
3 Quilts • 16 Techniques
Gail Searl

#1295 ............................ $12.95

**TRIANGLES at Play**
Bonnie K. Browning & Phyllis D. Miller

#1297 ............................ $12.95

**LOOK** for these books nationally.
**CALL** or **VISIT** our website at

# 1-800-626-5420
**www.LovetoQuiltCreations.com**